SEA

OF

Symphony

KAETLEN MUNDY

WESTBOW
P R E S S*
A DIVISION OF THOMAS NELSON
& ZONDERVAN

WestBow Press books may be ordered through booksellers or by contacting:

WestBow Press
A Division of Thomas Nelson & Zondervan
1663 Liberty Drive
Bloomington, IN 47403
www.westbowpress.com
844-714-3454

ISBN: 979-8-3850-0959-6 (sc)
ISBN: 979-8-3850-1003-5 (hc)
ISBN: 979-8-3850-0960-2 (e)

Library of Congress Control Number: 2023919510

Print information available on the last page.

WestBow Press rev. date: 11/13/2023

Dear readers, it's not done often enough, and I want you to know how appreciated you are. This one's for you, guys!

CONTENTS

PREFACE

Hello again, dearest friend.

I'll be honest: I never really know what to write here. You came for my poetry, my stories, yet I want you to wait just a little longer while I give you an entrance, a median of some sort, for you to stand on as you exit your waking world and enter my written one. The only problem is, I never really know what to write. Which, in hindsight, is rather ironic for a writer, to be fair.

I titled this section "Preface"—the before—simply because that's how I've seen many authors begin their works, though I believe the exact term "preface" is meant to give you some insight or information to help you learn about what you are about to read. But there is no information to share that most scholars would require in a book such as mine. Perhaps this section would have been more promptly titled "Before You Begin". Hmm. Something to consider for next time.

But if I must attempt to inform, then I shall. This book, my stories, are works that I have diligently put together over the last five years. The events of my life, the encounters I've shared with others, and the environment I live in are all factors in what my stories are about and are the reason they sit before you on paper today. However, while many of my stories have a clear message in mind, all are up to interpretation of some kind. I once told my sister that imagery and emotion were what poems were all about. If a writer cannot make you see the people or feel the emotions they are feeling as you read them, then we have failed in our efforts as writers.

That's why I am so glad you are here to read this. I want you to read it, love it, hate it, understand it, be confused by it, and everything in between. And then it is my most fervent wish that you tell me why. Please, if you are ever given the chance, tell me why you loved it or hated it. Tell me which story you connected with the most or which one confused you so much that you became angry with it. And I thank you now for simply just reading my work is the most joyous wish you could have granted me. Just the idea of you makes my heart feel lighter, regardless of what your opinion of it will become. So thank you.

Throughout this book, you will find evidence that I have been nervous and scared, thoughtful, with heart both heavy and light, and a lot on my mind. I believe most of my wonder and joy went into my last book, *Wings, Dreams, and Realities.* I wrote that book during my high school years, and you can tell just how much of a child I truly was if you go back and read it. This book, *Sea of Symphony,* is the first book I have written during my adult life. The first book I have made as a working-class citizen of my country. It may not be as dark as many poets seem to deem as appropriate for their works, but it certainly has a great deal more reality to it than my previous book could have hoped for. Regardless, I am proud of my work. Will there be times in the future when I may wish to go back and edit what has already been published? Yes, of course I will. Will I publish it anyway?

To never publish my work, regardless of how bad I may think it to be, would truly be an inaction I could never forgive myself for. And I refuse to let my regrets be the central focus of my being.

If I can take just another moment of your time, even if you don't want to read most of the stories in here, I encourage you to read the "Acknowledgments" at the end. It may not mean much to you, but to me, it means the most, that the people I have to thank receive the credit they are due. If nothing else, please read about them. That is all I ask.

Now, without further ado, welcome, my friend. Welcome to my *Sea of Symphony!*

I BREATHE, I AM

In the dark depths of the oceans I hide,
Embraced and warm with my heart beside.
I breathe, I am. Here in deep blue,
Consumed in part by the cobalt hue.

Confined, I can't. Where could I be?
I'd know my way could only I see.
I breathe, I am. Here down below.
Remembered lost. Where do I go?

Floating, I feel,
Forgetting what's real.
I breathe, I am. The ocean I hear.
So calm and tranquil, I do appear.

Screaming, I try, but I hear no voice.
Trapped am I, with no given choice.
I breathe, I am. Do what I can.
My life forgone when it began.

I breathe, I am.
I breathe.
I am ...
I breathe ...

Here in deep blue.
Trapped in part by the cobalt hue.
This is where in the dark I hide,
Embraced and warm, with my heart beside.

FIRST STOP

Finding west
Is what's best.
Right in the chest
Sits a northbound crest.
Trick or jest?
Sparrow's guess.
Time for the infant's rest
On Mother's breast.
Properly stopping when we find west,
Heading out on our new quest.
Evil Edgar under arrest.
Adding on some lemon zest.
Down at robin's nest
In vast new openness.
Never had guessed
Greg was shyest.
Watermelons digest,
Ever yummy greenest.
Still following dearest
Toward our wild west.

NO PEACE

Do you see it over there?
The flower that is
In bloom. It acts as if no
Darkness, no pain, no strife would ever dare to touch such
A delicate and innocent little thing.
It's almost as
If the little flower is declaring, "Be at peace."
If only
Such peace were true; but even the flower is only temporary.
For as every heart breaks,
So it is in
Nature; winter comes to continue the
Endless cycle
Of cold and warmth, of love, of
Life and death and chaos.

MOVE

"I'm so happy."

"Why?"

"I do not need to move."

"Why would you need to move?"

"I don't."

"But you just said—"

"I know what I said. I do not need to move."

"Why?"

"Because everything I need is here."

"Did you not want to move?"

"Too much work."

"What?"

"It's too much work to move! Too much energy wasted."

"Would you help me move, then?"

"Why would you need to move?"

"I don't. I am helping someone else move."

"Why would you do that?"

"Because I want to."

"Then you are a fool. That is too much work."

"They don't have much."

"So?"

"They need the help."

"Well, what would they do for me in return?"

"Be your friend."

"Ha! Friend. Rubbish. I don't even know them."

"You wound me. Are we not friends?"

"Of course we are. You help me when I ask."

"Well, they are my friends. Would you not help the friend of a friend?"

"Absolutely."

"Then you will come with me to help them move?"

"No."

"Why not?"

"Because I don't want to move."

"Then you have no friends."

SPRING

What is spring?
When is it?
It's not when the calendar says it is.
If the calendar was right all the time,
It wouldn't be so cold now.
I like winter.
But I'm tired of the cold.
What defines spring, anyway?
The budding trees?
The twitterpated creatures?
The green grass and blooming flowers?
Those can happen in summer, too, though.
So what is spring?
Where can I find it?
It's not under autumn's leaves.
Winter's snow holds no secrets,
If she snows at all.
But I like spring,
Just as I like summer and autumn and winter.
I miss spring.
But the calendar says she's here.
So why can't I find her?

A CHANCE

A whim, a fire, a blanket of life.
What follows this longing through endless strife?
A choice, a chance, a decision made final.
The answer: A list made longer than River Nile.

How wide, how far, how long does this go?
When all is done, what will I show?
Life will in, life will out.
What elements of the soul will come about?

This desert, a thirst, a trail not traveled.
The stars, a light, a history unraveled.
A whim, a fire, a blanket of life,
This longing that follows; what ends this strife?

WHY, INDEED?

Fist of anger
Spills my blood.
Gentle palms cup my cheek,
Wipe the blood from my face.
Shouts of wrath
Call my name,
While serene smiles
Light my face.
Fired eyes
Burn my flesh.
My heart cries,
"Forgiveness!"
Resolution clouds my blood
As sheer anger conquers theirs.
Gentle hands wipe the blood away.
"No more fighting," I say.
"Why? They have done everything to you.
Spilled your blood,
Called you names,
Burned your flesh.
Why would there be no fight when there is blood to be had?"
But no wrath fills this heart.
Only a longing for peace.
No war.
Love.
"Why?" is asked again.
"Why, indeed," I say, my last breath.

DOUBTFUL WHILE I WAIT

Doubt:
The feeling of uncertainty or lack of conviction.
Doubt:
Caused by fear, distrust, and anger.
Do I not trust in Him?
Am I afraid of Him?
Angry with Him?
He made us a promise so very,
Very long ago.
It's been nearly two millennia, I think.
And so much bad, so much darkness,
So much fear has come since then.
I believe in Him, the I Am.
The One Most High.
I do not hesitate when I say,
When I believe,
When I know my faith is in Him.
But still, I doubt.
When those I love get hurt,
When my health is at its worst,
When my wealth is at its lowest,
And my stomach caves because I have no food to eat.
When the nights are at their coldest
And even at their darkest;
When the day is blistering hot
And so bright I cannot see;
When I see all the people crying out with no answer to be heard;
When I see the pain we inflict on one another,
On the world;
When my children scream and cry;

When the elder sits lonely and forgotten,
I doubt!
Oh, I doubt
Because where is my God then?
Why does He not stop the pain, ease our hunger?
Why does He not give us warmth on the coldest nights
Or shade on the hottest days?
Why does He not answer when so many cry out His name
Or make all men equal in wealth and station,
As so many of our forefathers before have wished?
Why does He not heal the sick and dying
Or calm the frightened child?
Why does He not slay all wicked thoughts
from the murderer's mind
Or give strength to the plenty who are weak?
He made us so many promises so very, very long ago.
Nearly two millennia, in fact.
And still, He asks us to wait even longer.
And I doubt.
But not because of anger, no.
Not because I don't trust Him either, actually.
I am doubtful while I wait.
I doubt
Because I am afraid.

BURNING

Black. Flashing white.
Most crimson red. Deepest orange.
The world is burning
In a hue of blackest gray,
Yet I take not one step against it.
The ground shakes.
Cities topple; their buildings crumble.
Yet I do not turn away.
Rising smoke. Blurred vision.
A tidal wave of agony.
A pile of melted flesh
And crushed bones left forgotten.
All the world's creatures are dying.
I am dying.
Yet still, I do not raise my voice.
The world is burning.
Burning. Burning.
Dying.
But I have made no move to stop it.
Why?
The sun sets.
It rises.
The world will burn again.
Yet still, will I do nothing to stop it?

FAITHFUL

I am faithful

Even when I cannot explain.

SO YOU ASK ME ABOUT RACISM

So you ask me about racism.
Go ahead; I promise it's all right.
Just don't expect a normal answer
Since I'm a poet, and I'm white.

You see, racism to me
Doesn't make much sense.
Therefore, if you are racist,
I'm confused by your pretense.

You tell me about racism;
I tell you love is my only creed.
And in this truth, you must remember:
It is red that we all bleed.

To explain, I must remind you
We all are made of dirt.
The fact you don't remember that
Leaves me feeling quite disconcerted.

But I'm a woman, and I'm white,
So what do my opinions matter?
You judge me by my color;
Could anything be madder?

We are not so different, you and I.
Our color is not our character.
In my faith, you are my family.
I'm happier when we're together.

You now ask me my beliefs,
And I tell you my only truth is God,
The Lord of Lords and King of Kings,
And Jesus, His only Son.

With this faith, I have learned love
For all my fellow man.
This constant fight makes God weep.
What is this nonsense that you demand?

I will fight, but how I fight
Is like that of Martin Luther King.
With family and with faith,
Together we will sing.

Of many things I'm well aware,
Like the fact this ideal is naive.
But you asked me about racism,
So I told you what I believe.

I know you don't, but I hope someday—
One day—you'll understand.
And maybe when that day does come,
We'll see different fires throughout our land.

CAN YOU GUESS WHO I AM?

A roar so fearsome,
I am strength blinding.
I am the breath that's escaped from your lungs,
Weaving through the blades.
I am memories in a scent
Lost in the clouds.
I am cold that strikes the bones
And relief on your skin.
I am invisible.
I am a morning tune,
An evening dance,
A night's lullaby,
A song forever heard.
I am freedom unending,
The captor of wings.
I am the soaring eclipse
Of gray and white and gold and blue,
A touch of lavender,
And a stolen leaf or two.
Can you guess who I am?

WHEN I DREAMED

When I dreamed as a kindergartener,
I dreamed I'd grow to be as tall as the mountains,
Powerful and strong.
I dreamed of learning to walk on clouds
Like the angels and dragons
And of eating as much McDonald's as I pleased.

When I dreamed as a 4th-grader,
I dreamed of being a shapeshifter,
Of flying and crawling and growling,
Of being the "Cool Cat."
I dreamed of escaping school and homework
And out-facing all my classmates.

When I dreamed as an 8th-grader,
I dreamed the world was ending.
The sky was falling, the ground was shaking,
Fire and brimstone were all around.
I dreamed my bullies couldn't hurt me anymore
Because my crush and I were the only people left on Earth.

When I dreamed as a high school senior,
I dreamed of what college I would go to,
Of how much money I would make,
And who I would fall in love with.
I dreamed of how many children I would have
And the happily ever after that awaited me.

When I dream as an adult,
The details are very fuzzy;
I can't see them anymore.
I still have hope for children,
For a life without constant strife.
But where once I dreamed of the impossible,
Now, even what is real is beyond my reach.

THE TALE OF THREE

I want to tell a story I was told
About three triplets, with one so cold.
Another of the three was timid and shy.
The last one was adventurous, gracious, and kind.

The last triplet, so they say,
Was beautiful in every way.
But the other two never saw that fairness in the mirror.
Their luck on perfection would never be clearer.

And as they grew, their paths each one chose.
The cold one chose the path of the rose—
Solitary, quiet, content, and pleased.
This triplet followed through life with ease.

The adventurous triplet, full of beauty and grace,
Chose the path with a humbler pace.
They fell in love, their heart fulfilled.
The first triplet could not be more thrilled.

The timid one, as you've already guessed,
Is not the one who lived life the best.
Their heart grew bitter with each time they'd meet
The kindest sibling they'd never greet.

So, Wickedness grew in the timid one's heart,
And they wondered what would happen
should the kind one depart.
It would make my life better, that triplet thought with glee.
Perhaps I should see these events come to be.

But not alone, the once shy triplet knew.
Only together could the blow strike true.
So confide, they did, as everyone knows,
In the sibling that chose to follow the rose.

They plotted and planned; soon a chance they did seize.
Not once did the timid one sense the cold one's unease.
So when the time came for death to strike,
The cold triplet's blow fell a bit to the right.

The kind sibling's cry grew loud with grief
As their timid sibling's body crumpled like a leaf.
When the truth came out, everyone grieved,
For the cold one's story, only their sibling believed.

****

I want to tell a story I was told
About three triplets, with one so cold.
Another of the three was timid and shy.
The last one was adventurous, graceful, and kind.

So wicked was the cold one, so they say,
That they killed the timid sibling without delay.
The adventurous sibling, with cunning and aid,
To an early death was the cold one laid.

Then the kind triplet, full of passion and grace,
Chose the path with a much humbler pace.
They fell in love, their heart now healed,
A long life they lived, the triplets' fates sealed.

AMEN

When my soul is being torn apart,
And the Devil does his best to tear out my heart,
When I hold a new life in my hands with
more joy than all my days,
When hope floods in, in countless waves,
When to a crowd of millions I scream and cry,
And it seems like no one can hear me no matter how hard I try,
He hears me through it all
And is always there to answer my call!
When my tears fall like rain on grass,
And my smile becomes as fragile as a looking glass,
And not a soul seems to notice the pain I'm in,
Behind the mask I wear, which cracks from within,
When I raise my hands to praise His name,
Glistening tears falling, though not the same,
He sees my steady stream of tears
And wipes away the last of my fears.
When I have no voice to call me His,
And there's no one around to tell what is,
When I stand on trial before the gates,
Knowing the verdict for which hell does wait,
With redemption in sight, I have no hope left,
And the Devil's men reach for my flesh they've kept,
He speaks the word I long to hear
And brings me to a home in which He's near.
When I am frozen in darkness, my freedom lost,
Waiting for my turn to hang on the cross,
When the crowds call my name and shout for my blood,
The sin and death coming to drown me like a flood,
He moves to take my place,

Taking the grave and giving me grace.
He moves and sees and hears and speaks
From the oceans' depths to the mountains' peaks,
When I stood in darkness, in sin, in death, my end,
He became my Father, my Brother, my Redeemer, my Friend.
He is my God, my King, my Comforter, my Savior,
My Lord and life now and forever.
And even when I run, He comes again and again.
And because of Him, forever I will sing, "Amen."

I, A BURDEN BE?

I am a burden.
Never again will I believe
I will be enough.
My best efforts only give others grief,
And I'd be lying if I said
There are people who care about me.
I know without a doubt,
When I'm standing before the flames,
That I am alone.
How dare you say
My presence is appreciated!
How can you not know
Mistakes are my definition
I know it isn't true that
I am enough.
Never again will I hesitate to say
I can't.
Never again will I believe
I am not a burden.
(Read from bottom to top.)

I THOUGHT

I thought I was your sister,
The closest one to you.
I thought we told each other everything,
But I guess that isn't true.
I thought I understood you,
And that you knew me too.
But there were so many misunderstandings,
And we never talked them through.
I thought that we were friends,
Bound through sun and stormy weather,
But you rarely speak to me,
And we hardly talk when we're together.
I thought we had fond memories.
But the more I think about it,
Did we ever really know each other?
There's so much that I regret.
I thought I was your sister,
But I feel like I've been shot
So often that I've wondered
If our bond had been for naught.

FULL MOON, BLUE MOON

Full moon, full moon,
Shining so bright,
Half moon, crescent moon,
My guiding light.

New moon, new moon,
No longer can I see.
Crescent moon, half moon,
How frightening you be.

Blue moon, blue moon,
How rare to see your light.
Full moon, blue moon,
You make my night so bright.

YOUR MOTHER

~~~ᴍ~~~

Portions of the following story depict nondescriptive scenes of gun violence. Please use discretion upon reading, or skip over it if it makes you uncomfortable. The next poem is "Stride."

PART I

HOW THEY MET

"Hey, Daddy?"

"Yes, kiddo?"

"How did you meet Mama?"

"Well, that's a funny story, kiddo."

"Can you tell me about it?"

"Sure. I think you're old enough. Scooch over. Now see, I'll never forget the day your mother and I met. I was your average police officer, patrolling the streets one night, when out of nowhere, this car comes zooming past me like it's some NASCAR racer on the track. It wasn't a race car but was instead a red 2005 Ford, driving through a highly populated area. Now, that particular street may not have been a suburban neighborhood or a schoolyard, but anyone going that fast could still easily hurt themselves or somebody else. So I instantly turned on my lights and chased after them."

"And that person was Mama?"

"Oh, yeah. She didn't put up any fight or anything, either. The moment she saw my lights, she pulled right over and parked her car. Even waved to me when I stepped out of my car to talk to her."

"Did you arrest her?"

He laughed. "She never gave me a chance. The moment I walked up to her, she started rambling about how she needed to talk but didn't know who to talk to. She had gotten in her car and started driving around and eventually found herself going faster and faster. By the time I found her, your mother said she'd been praying for someone to stop her or pull her over before she hurt somebody. Your mother kept going on and on despite my attempts to calm her, eventually, she just broke down in tears and cried."

"Then you gave her a hug and kissed her all better like you do for me?"

"No, son. Comforting a crying adult is different from comforting your own kid, especially since I didn't really know your mama at the time. If I'd tried to kiss your mom then, I would have been punched in the face. And probably gotten a Taser to the groin. Your mother was quite the spitfire, so I wouldn't put it past her to do that even to me."

"Oh. So you can't just kiss everyone to make them feel better?"

"No. You can't go around kissing just anyone, especially strangers."

"Why not?"

"Heh, um. That's a story for another day, kiddo. Anyway, when your mother started crying, I asked her to get out of the car, and we sat on the curb together and talked."

"Just talked?"

"Just talked. I ... well, I learned that your mother had depression, kiddo."

"What's that?"

"It means she was really sad a lot of the time. But your mama was strong, and one of the toughest fighters I've ever known. The bad things just really got to her sometimes, and that day just happened to be one of those days. The sadness got your mother so badly she couldn't stand to stay in her home anymore. She needed to talk to someone, anyone, but didn't know who. So she took her keys, her Taser, and her phone, and went out driving until I pulled her over. And we sat, and I listened to her talk for hours."

"You listened to her? You didn't talk?"

"Nope."

"Why not?"

"Because, you see, son, I've learned through the years that with most people, and especially with people like your mother, they feel better and safer if they know they've been listened to. If you honestly make an effort to listen to someone's feelings and problems, not just talk to them, it helps that person in ways we cannot even imagine. Just knowing someone is listening makes a world of difference, kiddo. That's why we don't turn anyone away when they want to talk. Even a simple smile can change someone's whole day."

"And you changed Mommy's day?"

"That night? I helped your mama plenty, but that night, your mama changed my life forever, even if I didn't know it at the time. I listened to her talk for hours and hours, long past the time when my shift was over, but she felt much better once she got everything off her chest. I still had to give her a ticket, of course, but she was gracious about it. Ha! It was probably the first and only time I was ever thanked for giving someone a ticket!" Dad laughed.

"What happened next?"

"She got in her car and went home."

"Wha—?"

"And I went back to the station to finally finish my shift. I think I had to be driven home by a friend, though. We'd talked for so long, and it had gotten so late, I was practically asleep on my feet by the time I clocked out."

"Bu-But! You were supposed to ask Mommy on a date! Drive her home, give her a kiss!"

Pfft. And he laughed. "And what do you know about dating, kiddo?"

"I know plenty!"

"How so?"

"That's how the big kids at school say it goes."

"Big kids are still figuring out dating themselves. Take more advice from adults; we have a bit more experience. But yes, that was it. Your mama was speeding, I pulled her over to give her a ticket, we talked for a few hours, and then we went our separate ways."

"But you did go on a date, right?"

"Eventually. But that's a story for another day. Now it's time for you to go to sleep. You have school in the morning."

"But I want to—"

"No buts, kiddo. Time to sleep."

"Oh, okay. Will you tell me more about you and Mama?"

"Someday, kiddo. I love you."

"Love you, too, Daddy."

"Good night."

PART 2

THE FIRST DATE

"Hey, Dad?"

"Yes, kiddo?"

"How did you ask Mom out? I mean, what did you say when, when you asked her on your first date?"

"Why? Are you looking for some advice?"

"Wha—? No. What? No, I don't need advice on asking out a girl. What girl?"

"So there *is* a girl! Tell me more. Is she kind to you?"

"Dad, there is no girl. I'm asking about Mom! I'm allowed to ask about Mom, right?"

"Yes, yes, okay. I'll tell you about your mom. But only if you tell me more about this girl later, though. I only want the best for you, after all."

"Fine. Okay."

"Good. Now, do you want to hear about the events leading up to me asking your mother out or what we did on the first date?"

"Uh. Both? Both. Would probably help."

"Ah, oh. Heh."

"What?"

Dad laughed. "The events leading up to our first date may not actually help you much. If I hadn't been there myself, I would have said it was something straight out of a Hallmark movie. Well, no. Actually, it was a bit too intense to be in a movie like that. And I certainly don't wish that situation on anyone. Sweet Jesus, if you ever got in a pickle like that one, I might actually have a heart attack."

"What do you mean?"

"I … Well, uh, hmm …"

"Oh, come on, Dad! You can't just say stuff like that and then not say anything. That's rude, you know."

"I do know! I just don't know where to begin. Some days I still can't believe it myself."

"Well, just start at the beginning or something. When did you first see Mom again? After the ticket, I mean."

"Oh, well, that's easy only because it was pure coincidence. I stopped by a cafe on the way to my shift one evening, and she just happened to be sitting in a booth chatting with one of the baristas at the same time. Now, this happened a few months after we first met, so it took a while for us to recognize each other. But when we did, your mom was so thankful to see me again that she paid for my coffee."

"So Mom made the first move, then."

"Yes and no. Don't get all disappointed. Anyone can make the 'first move,' as you called it. You just have to have the courage to do so. This coffee, though, wasn't a date, kiddo. It was simply your mother trying to thank me for helping her in the only way she knew how at the time."

"Which one of you made the effort to get to know the other first then?"

"I … I guess we both did. Kind of."

"Dad, please hurry up and elaborate."

"It was confusing, okay? And a long time ago. Give your old man a break."

"You're not that old."

"Should I feel grateful for that comment or silly?"

"Dad."

"All right, already. Your mother insisted on buying me coffee. Wouldn't let me tell her no for even a second. We talked for a few minutes while the barista did her thing, but I still had to get going if I was going to get to work on time, so I turned to leave. I was halfway out the door when your mother asked me to wait. When I turned around to see her, that was when she asked me what my name was."

"Wait. You'd talked all that time, and you didn't even know each other's names?"

"You don't necessarily need to know someone's name to share a good talk with them, son. And no, I knew your mother's name, of course. I had been the one to give her a ticket and all. And your mother knew my last name since it was printed on my uniform. Mama simply wanted to know my first name, so she stopped me and asked."

"Was it really that important that Mom knew your first name?"

"For her? Yes. To this day, I still don't know why, but your mom said she had a feeling that day, so she acted on it. She asked me what my first name was, and I told her. And I'll never forget the look on her face when she heard what my name was."

"What was her face like?"

"At first she just blinked at me, like she didn't believe me. Even asked me to repeat myself. When I told her my name again, oh, her whole face lit up. Your mama's eyes went bright with the purest joy I'd ever seen on anyone's face, and the smile she gave me lit up the whole room. She held out her hand for me to shake, and something inside me just kind of clicked. I grew curious, you see. I wanted to know more about this woman who could smile so happily just from learning someone's name while also being so desperate at night that she'd go speeding down the road just to have someone to talk to. So I pulled out my card and gave it to her."

"The one with your contact info on it?"

"Yes, the very one."

"So wait, how is it that you both made the first move then?"

"Easy. Your mother was the one who bought me coffee and asked for my name, and I was the one who gave her my number."

"Wow. So I guess she called you then, huh?"

"Oh yeah. At ten o' clock the very next morning."

"And that's when you asked her out?"

"Nope."

"What?"

"Now son, I would hope you know me well enough by now to know that I'm not just about to ask a girl on a date simply because she smiled prettily at me the previous evening. No, she called me, and we just talked. We got to know each other better and quickly became good friends."

"Just friends? Seriously?"

"Yes, just friends. At first, anyway. You see, son, loves and crushes can come and go like the passing of the wind. Some of them you do take with you, and they can last a lifetime. But friendship—real friendship—is a lot harder to come by. And even harder to keep. And your mother and I weren't ready for a serious relationship at the time. Being a cop isn't easy, especially in our city, and your mom had her own stuff to deal with. Being a friend for each other helped."

"So wait. When did the date happen? You fell in love with her eventually, right?"

"Oh, I didn't really realize how much I loved her until years later. But I won't deny that my affection for your mother grew with each day I knew her. After about a year of being her friend, I decided I wouldn't mind dating your mom and wanted to talk to her about it to see if she felt the same. It was late one night, just after my shift ended. Your mom happened to be awake at the time, too, so we went to the cafe where we'd first formally met, and ... I'll be honest with you, son, that was one of the scariest nights of my life—for more than one reason."

"Why is that?"

"Well, for one, confessing one's feelings and leaving yourself open to others is no easy feat. I wasn't lying earlier when I said it takes courage to make the first move, and I was terrified! But for another ... Well, uh, oh, I'll just come out and say it. That night your mother took a bullet for me."

"She *what*?"

"She took a bullet that was meant for me. No sooner had we sat down at a booth with our drinks than a couple of college-age kids barged in with guns demanding the barista give them money. Your mother, as brilliant as she was, immediately ducked down to call 911 while I got up to get their attention away from the barista and maybe even talk them down. But these kids were high and not really thinking in their right minds. They didn't care what color skin I was or about the fact that I was dressed in civilian clothes. I walked and talked like the cop I am, and it made them nervous. So one of them took a shot. Your mother, though, she jumped in at the last possible second to push me out of the way. Took it right in her shoulder."

"I... I think I need to sit down."

"Yeah. You see now why I was so inarticulate earlier?"

"Yes. Yeah. It, uh, can't be easy telling a kid their mom got shot."

"No... No, it isn't."

"Mom was okay, though?"

"Oh yeah. She was a sight to behold, blood running down her arm. She'd crouched in front of me, protected me! Can you imagine? She had shouted so fiercely at the kids that they dropped their weapons and ran."

"You're kidding."

"I'm not. I had never been more scared in my life. Once the kids left, your mother just collapsed in my arms. She wasn't used to that kind of pain, you see. And who would be? The law enforcement finally came, along with an ambulance, and took your mom to the hospital, where she spent three days recovering because they had to go in and surgically remove the bullet embedded in her shoulder. I came to visit her at her home a week after that. I wanted to give her space, you know. And I asked her to date me right then and there."

"You just walked in and asked?"

"Well, not straightaway, of course. We sat and talked for a bit, like we always did. But that bullet had changed a lot of things for me. The first being that I now understood your mother was very important to me. I wanted her in my life, and the fact that she came close to not being in it was—"

"Scary?"

"Terrifying. The second thing was actually something I learned from experience on the job. Never hesitate, son. If you want to be with someone, never put it off until the next day. Don't waste your time thinking about the what-ifs because what's here today may not always be here tomorrow. I had known this before, but that experience made it a fact, so I acted on it. I asked your mom on an official date, and she said yes."

"What did you guys do?"

"We ordered pizza and watched a movie on her couch."

"That's it?"

"Yes. We didn't want to go out for the date. Couldn't really, between my work hours and your mom's injury. And we didn't want to make things more awkward than they already were, with us testing new waters in our relationship and all. So we kept it simple. I paid for the pizza, like the gentleman I am, and your mom chose the movie. It was wonderfully relaxing. And a month later, we began our official relationship."

"Huh."

"Is this helping any, son?"

"Yeah, I think so. I'm going to head up to bed now. Thanks, Dad."

"Anytime, kiddo."

"Hey, Dad?"

"Yeah?"

"Do you, ever, miss Mom?"

"Every day, kiddo. Every single day."

"Okay. I love you, Dad."

"Love you, too, kiddo. Good night."

"Good night."

PART 3

THE ARGUMENT

"Hey, Dad?"

"Yeah?"

"Did you and Mom ever fight? Argue?"

"Son."

"Yeah, okay. How did you handle the arguments, then? Did you ever yell?"

"Sometimes, yes. Did you and—"

"Yeah. We got into a, a pretty bad fight today."

"You want to talk about it?"

"I don't know. We started talking about our future today, since, you know, graduation is just around the corner and all. And we, well, disagreed, on what's the more important step to take next I guess."

"What is it you want to do next?"

"I want to settle, Dad. With her."

"You asked her to marry you?!"

"No! I, I simply brought up the idea, and she just, well, she just got all panicky and started yelling at me!"

"Do you blame her? Kiddo, do you really know what it means to marry someone?"

"Uh …"

"Yeah, I thought so. How much do you know about marriage?

"Two people take vows, exchange rings, and move in together. They start a family."

"I…Son, please tell me I didn't raise you to be that naive."

"What?"

"Marriage is so much more than that, son! Marriage is sharing each other's lives until your dying breath! It's, it's the ups and downs, the big things and little. It's love, son. It's a very serious thing, even if people often take it for granted. Do you understand, at least a little bit, kiddo?"

"I, I don't know. I think so?"

"But you still have questions."

"Yes."

"Do you want to hear about how your mother and I settled?"

"Please."

"Okay. We had been friends for three years, dating for two, when I asked her to marry me."

"How did you realize she was the one for you?"

"Little things. Well, one little thing in particular that topped it off, I guess. I had pulled a few tendons in my shoulder on the job one day. It took a surgery to get everything fixed. Your mom was there with me the whole time."

"That's not a 'little thing,' Dad. Surgery is something pretty big if you ask me."

"It is, and your mom was there for that. What I meant by the little things was the six weeks of recovery that followed and that your mother stuck around for."

"It couldn't have been that hard."

"It's a lot harder than you think. Sure, the first few days, maybe even the first week or so, can be easy. Especially when you still have pain medications running through your system. I was as loopy as a drunken sailor at times and said a lot of things I really don't remember that had your mom laughing so hard she cried. She managed to keep me in line during that time. But those pain meds don't last forever, and once the aftermath of your surgery kicks in, that's when things get hard. I was in pain all the time and in a sling that had so many—too many—latches on it. I had these gel packs that had to be frozen and placed in the sling with my arm every morning and then thawed and warmed to be placed before I went to bed. It was hard to move around easily. It was infuriating. I wore sweatpants for weeks because it was too difficult to button my pants with one hand."

"Mom didn't help you?"

"Not with the pants. I wouldn't let her even though we both

knew it wasn't sexual. That was one of the little things I loved about your mother. We were both very much attracted to each other on a physical level. I could never deny that your mother was beautiful, you know. But not once during that time did she ever try to make a pass at me. She honestly just wanted to help me because she wanted to. She never wanted anything in return."

"Is that when you knew for certain you loved her?"

"About that time, yes. But I lost my temper one day, kiddo. We both did about four weeks in. See, your mother had moved in temporarily to help take care of me, and it was the first time we'd spent nights together."

"By 'together,' you mean she slept in the guest bedroom, don't you?"

"As any gentleman should."

"But you never spent a night ... together?"

"Not until after we were married, kiddo. Not even when one of us was up there on medications."

"You don't think Mom would have tried something while you were loopy?"

"I knew she wouldn't. I trusted her as much as I trusted myself. It's one of the things that told me she was the one for me. If you can't trust the ones you love, then you're not aiming for a happy ending."

"Huh. What happened after you lost your temper? You said you both had."

"Oh yeah. Like I said, it was the first time we'd spent nights in the same house together for even one night, let alone six weeks. You learn a lot about a person in those few weeks, learn just what kind of person they are behind closed doors."

"And what kind of stuff did you learn?"

"Well, for one, your mother loved to sing."

"Sing?"

"Oh yeah. All the time. It was one of the things that helped to calm her down the most. Sang all the time, in all different kinds of ways. Sometimes a hymn, sometimes a top-20 chart list, depending on what there was, of course. Sometimes she'd even sing in different languages if she felt in the mood for it."

"And she did it all the time?"

"Once she felt comfortable around me, yeah. Started out with humming random tunes here and there, and eventually, it became almost like a full concert, but only singing songs that meant something to her."

"Was she any good?"

Dad laughed. "That also depended on what mood she was in, sometimes. Getting emotional can make it hard to carry a tune. But I got really annoyed with her at first. The singing got on my nerves after the first couple of days."

"What did you do?"

"I asked her to stop."

"And did that work?"

"Not, well, not in the way you'd think."

"What do you mean?"

"I asked her to stop, and she did. That was just the kind of person your mother was—accommodating of others—but I shouldn't have done it. Not when it was at her expense."

"Why not?"

"Because I took away a part of who your mother was. Singing came to your mother as easily as breathing, and I shouldn't have asked her to quit. And though it was unintentional, I also made your mother's depression worse by asking her to quit."

"How?"

"Your mother was strong, kiddo. She managed to keep her depression in check, give or take an episode or two, but she needed her outlets to help her manage it."

"And one of those outlets was singing."

"That's right. Your mom always said that if given the choice between singing and screaming, most people prefer to hear the singing. You cause less panic that way. And by making her stop her singing, I pushed your mom into an early episode of depression. I made her think … I made her think she wasn't good enough. Ah mind you, it wasn't just the absence of song that caused your mama's lapses. It's really a lot more complicated than that."

"I know, Dad. It's okay. I've read about it. What did you end up doing in the end?"

"We exploded, for lack of a better term. Your mom was experiencing the worst of an episode, and thanks to my irritation with her singing, she didn't feel as though she could confide in me this time. Her emotions came to a head, and I got angry at the eventual outburst because I hadn't seen the signs for it like I had before. I was so ashamed when I realized. Once the fighting was done, I told her to sing again. I almost begged for it after a certain point, and I learned to live with it. It wasn't too long after that when I actually learned to look forward to it. She had a beautiful voice. But that's just the thing, son. I loved your mother, and loving her meant accepting her for who she was. I had to accept the singing, all the knickknacks she loved to collect. I accepted her depression and treasured the times I could make her really laugh. We loved each other, and that eventually meant having to deal with the dirty laundry and the pileup of dishes. It meant working through the late nights and early mornings. Our schedules conflicted a lot, particularly in those early days, so finding quality time together was more difficult than I make it sound."

"And the arguments?"

"Marriage means that no matter how big or how bad an argument gets, you still come back and work things out. That's what happened that day a few weeks after my surgery. We had our first big fight, with lots of yelling and things we both regretted saying. So your mother walked out."

"She left?! Just like that?"

"She came back, though. Always did, every time. It took me about half an hour to realize how wrong I'd been, how wrong we both were. I rushed to the door to go after her only to find her sitting on my front porch with two hot chocolates in her hands. She'd marched her way to the little gas station down the road to get us some drinks and then came right back. And then she waited for me to come back too. Just like she knew I would."

"How did she know you'd come back to her?"

"Because if you really, truly love someone, son, you'll come back to them every single time. That was the moment your mother and I both knew we loved each other so much. It was the moment I knew I wanted her to be my wife."

"But what if you yell at each other? What if... what if you say things the other can't forgive?"

"It may take a while, but you can still find your way back to her. And she to you. Your mother and I once got in a spat so bad it was nearly a whole week before we could even stand to look at each other. But we made it through because I was your mother's and she was mine, and our actions spoke much louder of that than our words ever could."

"Oh."

"Son, is she willing to come after you? Do you want to go after her?"

"I don't know... But, I want to try."

"Good. Do you still want some advice?"

"What else do you have?"

"More than you, kiddo. When you two get to talking again, take it slow. Both of you are barely adults. Don't try to argue it. I was still a kid myself practically until the day I turned thirty. And you're still trying to figure out what you want to do in your life. She is too. I know you want a family, son, and I am so proud of that. But make sure you're not jumping into the ocean before you learn how to swim. It won't be easy, but take your time, so you can provide for your family when you do have them. And make sure the both of you are on the same page. It won't do to be in a relationship where you both can't do what you both want. It's not healthy. Promise?"

"Okay, Dad. I promi—...Dad, Dad! She's calling me! She's on the phone. She's really calling!"

"I think that answers one question then. All right, son. Go on up to your room so you can talk to her in private. Let me know how it goes. Just remember, take it slow, talk to her, and make sure you listen to her too."

"Okay! Okay. Thanks, Dad. I'll talk to you in the morning. Love you!"

"Love you too, kiddo. Good luck!"

"Thanks again, Dad! Good night!"

"Good night."

PART 4
LIFE

"Hey, Dad?"

"Yes, son?"

"How did, um, how did Mom die?"

"Kiddo, if you're worried about your wife and baby, it's all right. You got them here in time, and the doctors here know what they're doing. They're in good hands."

"I know that. I know. It's just, the baby's come early, really early. And I, I'm trying to stay positive, but I can't help but think—"

"They're going to be just fine."

"You can't know that."

"I do know that."

"How?"

"Cause I went through the exact same thing with you and your mother."

"Really?"

"Oh yeah. Scared me half to death. You weren't due for at least another four weeks, and your mom decided to visit the precinct to share a late dinner. Now, I'm sure you know how those midnight cravings go."

"Oh yeah."

"Well, you can imagine the look on my face when your mother's water broke right there in the middle of the precinct. I nearly had a heart attack. Things got complicated once we got to the hospital, and they sent me out to the waiting room, just like they're doing with you right now. But you both turned out just fine. Perfect, even."

"You're being biased, Dad. Nobody's perfect. Not even a newborn."

"I know that. But trust me, kiddo. The second you walk into that room and see your wife and baby, nothing will ever be more perfect than that moment."

"I don't know. The day I saw my wife walking down the aisle might contend with that."

"Ha! That it will, son. That it will."

"...So, Mom didn't, die in childbirth?"

"...No, she didn't. You really want to talk about this now?"

"I honestly don't know when I'll have the courage to ask again, Dad."

"It's not, really, a matter of when you have the courage to ask, son... It's a matter of if I have the courage to tell you."

"Then at least tell me this, please. You, you always talk about Mom's depression, knew she had it long before she'd even met you. I, I've studied depression, Dad, you know I have. I even help other people who have it too. But not everyone can cope with depression well, and in some extreme cases—"

"Don't. Kiddo, just don't. I've told you about your mother, told you how strong she was. She had depression, yes, but she fought it. I cannot stress to you just how long, how hard, and how often she fought it. But there was too much love in her heart for her to lose that battle, and she would never have left us like that. Never. So don't ever think that was an option for her. I-I'm sorry I left you alone long enough to even entertain the idea."

"So Mom didn't ... take her own life?"

"No, son. She loved you, loved life too much to do something like that."

"Okay... okay. That's, okay, that's all I needed to know. Thank you, Dad, for at least telling me that. I don't, I don't need to hear anymore."

"...Yes, you do."

"What?"

"She was your mother. You deserve to know what happened to her. I just, I never knew when a good time was to tell you. I just didn't want to raise you with fear or anger in your heart. Your mother, she wouldn't have wanted that, so I kept putting it off. But, you're about to be a father now yourself, and you've already been raised by a cop, so you know what it's like living in any kind of association with a police officer. It shouldn't be too hard... No, it'll always be hard. I'm sorry, son, I just—"

"It's okay, Dad. Just take a deep breath, and... start from the beginning, I guess."

"Okay. Um, well, you know how it is, kiddo, with social media, how it often portrays law enforcement. Though I won't deny that some of what they say is true, it often doesn't matter what you do as an officer. Somehow, you'll always be the bad guy."

"Yeah?"

"Yes. Being a cop, you ruin people's chances of a happily ever after. You take away some people's livelihoods when you stop a drug dealer, tear apart families when you have to report someone's loved one is a murderer, a thief, or has been found dead. One of your fellow officers accidentally shoots the wrong kid; or your chief makes one bad call, and within twenty-four hours, the world's more than willing to watch you burn at the stake... Doesn't matter how much good you've done or how many people you help, somehow your entire career always boils down to one wrong decision and often the color of your skin."

"One bad apple means the whole barrel burns, right?"

"Right. Now I can't, I won't, deny that there are bad cops out there. I'm well aware that there are individuals out there who will abuse the power the badge gives them. There have been a few in my own precinct- God knows, I've made a few decisions myself that I'm none too proud of. But that doesn't mean we're all bad or that, at the end of the day, we can't at least still be considered good people. But people listen to whatever the media tells them, so a majority of good cops are placed under the same mantle the bad ones are, and society tends to forget you as an individual."

"Where are you going with this, Dad?"

"Your mother, your mama was a cop's wife. And she was very proud of that, proud of me. She had the bumper stickers all over her car, even had a little flag hanging from her car antenna. She fought for us, kiddo. Not all cops, mind you. Your mom said she couldn't fight for all cops 'cause she didn't know all cops. But for me, for the men and women down at the station, the people we considered our family, she was our loudest and strongest supporter. The constant riots made her depression worse, not just because we officers had to go out there to handle it, but also because lives were being taken unnecessarily."

"But, weren't the riots—"

"More innocent people were hurt during those riots than the people deemed guilty. No, the riots were hurting more than they were helping, so your mama spoke out against them. She wanted to make peace like Martin Luther King Jr. did. A lot of people, they didn't understand that."

"Dad, I, I don't like where this is going."

"You were at a toddler age when it happened. Barely more than a baby. It was dead of winter, late one night, but we were low on groceries. It was my night off, so I stayed home with you while she left. She, she never came back."

"What happened?"

"It, it was a hate crime, son. Your mother, she was stopped at a stoplight. I told you about her bumper stickers. Everyone with eyes knew she supported us cops, and anyone watching local news might have seen her standing up for us. And, and the rioters didn't take too kindly to that. She got boxed in by a gang waiting at the light. Words were exchanged. I think one of them recognized her from a rally or two. They... they shot her, in the head and chest, eight times. Then they set her car on fire. I got the call a few hours later. Your mama was, she was gone."

"W-Why? Why would they?"

"They thought they were bringing justice to the families that lost someone to a cop. That somehow killing her would make everything right."

"I, uh—"

"I'm sorry, son. I'm so sorry."

"Dad—"

"I know, kiddo. I'm sorry."

"...Did, uh, did you, uh, ever catch the guys who did it?"

"Yes. Nearby surveillance cameras caught the whole thing on tape. Didn't take us long to arrest them."

"What did you do? When, when you caught them?"

"I wasn't part of the arresting party; the chief didn't want me to do something I'd regret. But when I heard the arrests were successful, I, I became so angry. They took my wife—your mother—away from me. They showed her no mercy, treated her so cruelly, I wanted them to hang. I wanted to see them to the electric chair myself. I became so hateful, so vengeful, I went to the detention center to confront them. I was ready to yell, scream, fight. A couple of the guys walked down with me to make sure I didn't try something."

"So you met them, the guys who did it?"

"Yes."

"What did you do?"

"...I wore my uniform when I went to see them. I had wanted to show them that the full force of the law was coming to get them, no questions asked. But I walked into the cell, and the first thing they did was call me a traitor."

"What?"

"Yeah, can you believe that? I heard that, and something inside me just, broke. All my anger, the hatred I'd built up, just left me. All I was left with was an overwhelming sense of grief. I hadn't cried yet, during that time after your mother died. It hadn't felt real, that she was really gone. I spent weeks watching the front door, just waiting for her to walk through it and yell at me to help her with the groceries. But in that moment, when I was called a traitor, it all just came crashing down on me. I fell to my knees right there in the cell, and I cried. I don't, I don't quite remember what happened after that. Things became, hazy, after I finally allowed myself to grieve. Later, my partner told me I left everyone crying—the perpetrators included—because in my gut-wracking sobs, the only thing I said was 'She was my wife, she was my wife.' ...They ended up having to drag me out of the cell, and someone then drove me home. Someone handed you to me, and I, I just held you and cried until I couldn't cry anymore."

"Oh, Dad."

"I asked the judge, when the trial came, to not give them a death sentence. Their deaths wouldn't have made your mother happy, and it certainly wouldn't have given anyone justice. They're in a jail cell now, sentenced to life in prison, with no parole.

"I'm sorry I never told you before, son. I wanted to raise you the way your mama would have wanted. She always fought to see the best in people and never wanted any of her children to see the world as only black and white. 'There's a shade of gray for everything,' she always said, and she strove to show others that balance as well. I wanted to teach you the same things, give you the life she would have wanted for you if she hadn't—. It wasn't perfect, but I, I tried my best, I think. And it wasn't right, but telling you the truth before now—"

"I understand, Dad. Really. It's okay."

"It's *not* okay, son. You know that."

"Yeah, you're right... It's not okay. But it's okay to not be okay. I may never fully understand what you had to go through."

"I pray you never do."

"But I know why you didn't tell me until now. Thank you, for finally telling me."

"Your mother loved you, kiddo. I hope you know that we both love you so much."

"I know, Dad. I know. There are some things I regret her not being here for too, but you did your best. I know you did. And I'm, I'm so, so proud to call you my dad."

"Come here, kiddo." They embraced for a long time.

"...Look, son, they're calling you now. Your baby's here."

"The baby! I, I've got to— Will you be—"

"Go to them. I'll be fine. I'll follow behind you after I let the guys at work know how things went."

"Okay. Uh, you know what room, right? Have they said what room yet? Oh no. Oh no, no, no. I can't remember what room they're in. What if I can't find them, I—"

"Whoa, slow down, son. Take a deep breath. That's it. See that nurse over there who's calling your name? He'll take you right to where your family is. Go on. I'll be right behind you."

"Okay. I'll, uh, see you in a few minutes then. Okay, Dad?"

"Sure thing. Go enjoy that perfect moment."

"Okay."

***

"Hey, son, how are—"

"Shh, Dad! She's asleep. They both are."

"Oh sorry. I forgot how exhausting labor can be for the ladies."

"She did so good though."

"So how was it, seeing them for the first time?"

"You were right, Dad. I've never seen something so beautiful in my life."

"Told you so. Now, how's my grandbaby?"

"Breathtaking. Here, Dad. I want you to meet your granddaughter."

"Oh, son. She's beautiful."

"Good thing she takes after her mother, huh?"

"Hey, we boys aren't that bad looking, either, you know."

"I know. Would you like to hold her?"

"I don't want to wake her up."

"If my crying didn't wake her up, I doubt her grandpa holding her will make a difference."

"If you're sure."

"I'm sure. Okay, baby, up we go. Here, sweetie, this is your grandfather."

"Hi there, baby. I, I'm your grandpa… so beautiful, sweetheart."

"You okay, Dad?"

"Yeah, son. I'm just so proud of you, both of you. And I'm still trying to wrap my head around the fact that my baby boy's a daddy now."

"Yeah, I'm still trying to get used to that myself."

"It'll hit you one day.... She'll be running around the house, full of spitfire energy just like her mother's, and call you 'Daddy,' and it'll hit you. She'll call for you when, when she falls down and look to you for hugs when she's sick. She's going to demand you help her with her homework and put up a fuss when you tell her it's her turn to do the dishes. One day, you'll see her to her first day at school and get so protective when she finally starts dating. You'll be the shoulder she cries on when her heart breaks. You'll be one of the first people she turns to when she needs some advice, and you'll stand tall and proud, so proud, when she graduates with her diploma in hand. Then someday down the line, you'll be there to see her walk down the aisle with the most brilliant smile plastered on her face. You'll see her get sad and confused and angry, excited, scared, and happy, knowing the entire time just how much she's loved every moment of her life, and you'll know. You'll know you're her daddy."

"Hey, now... My daughter's only just been born. Don't try to marry her off already."

"Watch out, kiddo. That day will come a lot quicker than you think."

"Nope, not happening."

Dad chuckled. "Don't make me laugh like that, or I really will wake her up. Now, um, your in-laws should be on their way, right?"

"Yeah. I texted them just before you came in. They managed to secure a flight in the morning, so they'll be here sometime tomorrow afternoon. Might even help us get home, since the doctors should discharge the girls—my girls, can you believe that?—from the hospital by then."

"I'll leave you to spend time with them, then, tomorrow. But I've got to warn you, the guys at the station want to throw a party for you three sometime in the next couple weeks, especially now that they'll know the official gender of the baby."

"Oh boy."

"I'm trying to talk them down from doing anything too extreme since you've only just had the baby and all. But you know how they are."

"As long as we don't have a repeat of my twenty-first birthday, I'm sure it'll be fine."

"We'll keep them in line, somehow. Here, you've all had a long, exhausting day, so I'll leave you to rest. If you need any help, any kind at all, you know how to get hold of me. For now, just enjoy some quality time with your wife and baby girl."

"Okay... Hey, Dad?"

"Yeah?"

"We, we've talked about it, did talk about it, and decided months ago. Even before today, we had the name chosen for both a boy and a girl, so don't think our talk today is the only thing influencing it. We—"

"What, son?"

"We decided that if we had a boy, then we'd name him after our dads. And, since we had a girl, we decided to name her after Mom—both our moms really—but she's going to carry Mom's name with her. We decided to honor our parents by naming our kids after them, to remember you by, and—Dad, you okay?"

"Yeah... Yeah, I'm okay. I'm just, remembering that I really am a daddy."

"Oh Dad."

"Come here. I love you, son, so much. I'm so proud of you."

"I love you, too, Dad. I'll, uh, I'll see you soon?"

"Of course. Get some rest now. I love you."

"Love you, too, Dad. Good night."

"Good night."

PART 5

GOODBYE

"Hey. Dad? ...You don't have to say anything. I, I know. You're going to go see Mom soon... Aren't you?"

"She's kept me... waiting a long time, you know."

"Do you think you could wait just a little bit longer? The others will be here soon. It's just a couple more hours."

"Don't think ... I can wait that long ... kiddo."

"Dad-"

"Shh, shh. Come here, baby boy."

"...How did you manage it? After Mom died."

"I grieved, I told you. I grieved for months, years... But your mama taught me to love the little things—even in the face of grief, fear, and anger ... It still hurt. A lot. Always hurt after I lost her. But I remembered ... Had so many good, good memories together ... so I still loved the little things, like you."

"I think I was hardly a 'little thing,' Dad."

"Were when I first held you. So tiny ... thought I'd break you. But you kept growing ... got so strong. So much like your mama ... so much."

"You were right, you know. About kids growing up fast. My baby girl's going to be in college soon. Can you believe that? She's, she's really excited to show you her acceptance letter."

"So smart ... Always loved so much."

"Um, uh, the boys are getting big too. They're both in high school now. One of them's even got himself a girlfriend now too. You, you might remember her; you've met a couple of times. She fits right in with the family, even, even before she started dating my boy."

"Missed so much ... baby boy. My boy."

"I ... uh, I'm ... I don't know what to say, Dad,"

"Shhh. Shh. Mama, be home soon, so soon."

"Dad…"

"My boy, hold them close."

"What?"

"Your forever …"

"Oh, Dad…"

"Love you … so much."

"I love, I love you too, Daddy. So much. So, so much."

"…"

"Dad?"

Silence was the only reply.

"Good night."

STRIDE

Once, my doubts crept in,
And I begin to ponder why,
When a point on my brow feels sharp and cold.
Upward, my eyes turn
To find the piercing silver-gray of the sky.
Another pin prick on my cheek—
A droplet, a tear?—slides down,
And the sky begins to weep.
Not long, it is, before the chill sets in,
A welcome respite.
So not once does my pace quicken.
Moments pass.
My feet slosh through puddles.
My fingers become unfeeling.
But again, my strides remain unchanged.
Silver skies give way to smoky gray,
Which then becomes a hollow black,
And my strides remain the same.
The water stops.
The cold remains.
I am numb.
My strides remain the same.

OKAY

To not be okay
Is okay.
Never forget
You are strong.
Crying is not weakness;
Crying is courageous.
You are strong,
So let it out.
Let it all flow over you,
Like water over a stone.
I can't tell you it will be all right.
I can't tell you it's going to be okay.
All that I can say is
For right now,
Right this very moment,
It's okay
To not be okay.

THE RED SCARF

Once upon a time, I lived in Kentucky. As the oldest of my siblings, I have the most memories of the time we lived there. I remember the street addresses we lived at and the route we took to school. I remember the church we attended and the names of all the animals that lived on our street. I remember the rainy days and the little snow we got in the winter. And I remember the tornadoes that we lived through. In particular, I remember the aftermath of the tornadoes, when our parents would bustle us kids into the car, and we would go and see what destruction the disaster had caused.

Specifically, there was one storm that had torn apart a county not far from ours, and my parents wanted to see just how bad the damage was. Driving past, we saw there had been a house where nothing was left but a single wall. No windows, no furniture, not even the front door was left, just debris. My parents kept wondering what might have happened to the people who lived there. Another house fared much better; it only lost a corner of the house, so you could see into the master bedroom and kitchen even from the road as we drove by. After the damage had been surveyed and commented on, my parents began to drive us back home, and I looked up. To this day, I cannot tell you why I looked up or what compelled me to do so. I was only eight or nine at the time this tornado had hit, so maybe you can chalk it up to satisfying my childlike curiosity.

Regardless, I looked up at the treetops out my car window on the way home and spotted a long red scarf wrapped around a branch and blowing in the wind. I saw the scarf for only a few seconds, but the image of it was one that is still with me today. I always wonder about it, about the symbolism and meaning behind it. Some might say it was waving farewell, signaling the loss of something, or something poetic like that. More logic-based people would know that it was just another thing displaced by the tornado from the night before. The fact that it just happened to land in the tree was pure happenstance, so it doesn't mean anything. I, however, am not like most people, poetic or realist. Because whenever I think of tornadoes, that scarf always comes to mind, and it gives me hope. Every time I saw that scarf in my mind's eye, I would see a girl. A lost teenage girl swept up by the storm, and left in a tree far from her home.

I never know who she is, or why I keep seeing her when I think of the scarf, but she's always there. You see, this girl lived in one of the houses that got razed by the tornado and, left alone in the house that night, hid in the bathtub to keep away from the storm. Obviously, hiding in the bath doesn't do much good when the tornado hits you head-on, but it was enough to keep the girl in one piece long enough for the storm to pass. And passed it did, after carrying her hundreds of miles from home and then dropping her in a tree. The severity of her injuries, I'll leave to your imagination. The only thing I know with absolute certainty is that she had a head injury that caused severe memory loss. She awoke the morning after the storm still in the tree, like Disney's Dumbo after his drunken flight.

As I said before, the girl was injured but able to climb down the tree on her own. According to the story, it sometimes takes two days, sometimes a week, but she manages to make it to a road where someone found her and took her to a hospital. Her head injury left her with no memory of her life before waking up in the tree, so the police, once called, could only speculate on where she came from. Though the possibility of her being someone lost in the storm was discussed, the girl's profile didn't match any missing persons in neighboring counties. And two states over, her parents and two siblings were certain the girl was dead. They had searched for their daughter and sister, of course, but with their family photos gone, no access to phone chargers, and their passwords only saved in their phones, they had no picture to add to their missing person's poster.

When a search on the missing person's boards yielded no results, investigators began looking into the possibility of the girl being an escaped kidnapping or human trafficking victim. In theory, it would explain what she was doing so far in the wilderness with the injuries she'd sustained. And if she'd been so badly injured while trying to escape her captors, climbing up a tree to evade them would have been the only intelligent, if not risky, move she could have made. Her memory loss could have then been the result of both trauma and her injuries. More investigation was done, and though officers did find evidence of people living in abandoned cabins around the area, there was no evidence linking the girl to any particular site.

The girl, meanwhile, had been trying to sort things out for herself. Once seen by doctors, they could only verify that she was roughly sixteen or seventeen years old, so technically, still a minor. With no family stepping forward to claim her, the police had taken her into their custody while conducting their possible human trafficking theory, only to practically drop her when that investigation yielded no results. Her case was labelled unsolved, and the girl was sent into the foster system. She then ended up in the care of one of the nurses who attended to her during her recovery. The nurse and the girl had bonded quickly, and it was soon time for the two of them to think about the girl's future.

Being so late in her teenage years without a memory meant that school was difficult for the girl. The nurse ended up hiring a tutor from the nearby high school to help the girl through her studies, and through the tutor, the girl established a friend group. These teens heard the girl's story and all but adopted her into their group, helping her through high school as best they could. They held study groups once the girl had joined their class to help each other through semesters, and the girls in the group held sleepovers so that the girl felt included. While the nurse encouraged the girl to try different hobbies to see if one may trigger a memory for her, the teens took great pleasure in introducing the girl to their favorite movies, sports, snacks, and other things.

It took time for the girl to get used to everyone. Having people around who genuinely seemed to care about her helped the girl get through the nights when she felt like less of a person without her memories. When the police had no choice but to drop her case, leaving her as unknown Jane Doe, the nurse had taken a weekend off and stayed home with the girl, comforting her and spending time with her when she needed it. Once the holidays came around, the girl's friends gifted her with things they learned she might like to cheer her up. The gift she loved the most ended up being a red scarf the nurse had gifted to her after noticing she liked that color best.

Miles and miles away, the girl's family buried an empty casket and grieved for their lost daughter and sister. They attempted to carry on and did their best to live their lives knowing she wouldn't come home. At the same time, the girl worked toward graduating high school and planned on attending university with one of her closest friends in pursuit of getting a degree in psychology. Having learned quickly that the girl had an intense fear of storms, the nurse had wasted no time in getting the girl a therapist for her unknown PTSD. And through continued interactions with her therapist, the girl not only learned to live an emotionally stable life but also found respect for psychological therapeutic practices. So she grew to want to learn how to help others like her with their fears and became a licensed therapist.

Call it what you want, but the girl, now a woman, fell in love and got married. The man who would end up giving his heart to her was an older brother of one of her high school friends. Because he knew her past, it was easier for the woman to open up to him, so when fleeting interactions turned into late-night phone calls, it didn't take much for the woman to agree to a date. When he asked for her hand in marriage, the nurse who took her in was the one to walk her down the aisle. The couple spent a few years working out their dynamic before adopting a child as their own. The woman gave birth to two more children in the years following.

Now, most would assume this is where the story of the red scarf ended. The woman, now grown, was able to forge ahead and create a happy and successful future for herself despite her memory loss.

However, I should once again remind you that I am not like most people.

Though the woman had come to terms with her past and found joy in the family she found, there was still one person not satisfied with the ambiguous ending: her little sister. One of the blood relatives the woman had forgotten grew to be a very ambitious woman, a lawyer, and she still wanted answers. You see, the little sister was getting ready to be married, and looking at the guest list for her wedding often made her think of her lost sister. Oh, her parents had been able to grieve and eventually move on, and her brother had gone through a rough patch before getting himself back together. But the little sister felt stuck. They'd never found a body for her sister, and there had never been any real closure outside the empty casket buried six feet down.

It was something that had sat heavily on the little sister's mind throughout her childhood—this likely false hope that maybe—just maybe—since a body never turned up, the girl they'd mourned for so many years could still be alive. This hope was what the little sister now clung to so far into her adult life. And now that she was getting ready to be married, she wanted to know what really happened to her sister. And so on an impulse, she hired a private investigator—a PI—to look into the disappearance and if possible, the whereabouts of the girl lost in the tornado. It was a reckless move, one that only the little sister's fiancé knew of and did not fully support, but it was what the sister needed. Good or bad results, she wanted to move into her marriage without clinging to the grief and confusion of her adolescence.

The investigator, once hired, began his search. He started by looking into any "persons found" cases matching the girl's age and description in the area where the family used to live. When, of course, the search turned up nothing, the PI began following the route of the tornado during that storm. With the technology made available today, it wasn't hard to do. The investigator looked through the list of people found in each area the tornado passed through until he had a list of individuals matching the girl's profile. Keeping the little sister updated on his progress, the investigator booked a flight, rented a car, and travelled to see if one of the women was his client's sister. After much trial and error, the investigator eventually found the hospital where the girl was admitted and the nurse who took her in.

The nurse was reasonably surprised when a man showed up at her workplace asking about her adopted daughter. After learning the man was hired by the woman's blood sister and confirming the woman's identity, the nurse still refused to give any information to the PI. She knew how much this meant to the woman she had raised, but the nurse also knew the woman was finally happy, and learning this new information about her blood family after all these years would put that happiness at risk. The well-being of her daughter and her grandchildren was not something the nurse was going to chance, so she flat-out told the PI that yes, his client's sister was alive, and yes, she was doing well in life. But if the little sister wanted to know anything more about the woman, she would have to speak to the nurse directly.

Seeing that the nurse was not going to budge on the matter, and knowing that he had, in fact, accomplished his assignment, the PI wrote down the nurse's contact info at her request and returned to his client with the news. The little sister's reaction to hearing that the girl was alive is different every time I think about it, because how exactly is one supposed to act when you find out your long-thought-dead sibling is, in fact, alive and happy but has no memory of you? It was only thanks to the professional lawyer inside the little sister that she didn't completely break down and call everyone to let them know the girl was alive. As it was, she sat with her fiancé, and discussed what to do now that they knew the truth.

The girl that the little sister knew was now a grown woman. She had a foster mother who loved her like her own, a husband who treated her right, kids she adored, and a career she could be proud of that also let her provide for the family she loved. The woman had a different name and a different life from the one the little sister remembered of her. They were strangers. Of their blood family, their parents had managed to create a new sense of normalcy for their family after the girl's believed death and were living life as best they could with their two remaining children. Their older brother was on his way to being fully sober and even had a child and girlfriend now. The little sister herself was looking forward to getting married. Knowing what she did, telling the woman about her blood family or vice versa would do nothing but disrupt everyone's lives. It would dredge up old feelings and create a new storm inside all of them that could cause more harm than good. There wasn't even a guarantee that things would work out with the woman, and knowing that their daughter was alive but unwilling to speak to them? That would break her parents' hearts.

The little sister, she just couldn't do that to her family.

So the little sister contacted the nurse and asked all the questions she was allowed. The nurse did her best to answer her questions patiently. They talked for many hours during the initial phone call and then via email in the weeks that followed. Discussions involving the girl and her family's lives following her disappearance cemented the notion between the nurse and lawyer that the woman's true identity should remain a secret. Once satisfied that the woman lived a healthy and loved life of her own, the little sister asked only one more request of the nurse: She wanted to invite the nurse and the woman to her wedding.

On hearing the invitation, the nurse was greatly concerned. After all, the two women had just spent so much time discussing why involving the woman with her blood family would be a bad idea, but the little sister was insistent. Aside from the family of the bride and groom, who would be seated in the front row, there was no assigned seating at her wedding. The little sister and her fiancé felt their union should be of a combined family instead of separated . So, with the large number of invited guests and the lack of assigned seats, no one would be able to properly tell who the woman came for. As the bride, the little sister would go around to the reception tables, greeting and thanking the out-of-town attendees, but main family and friends would stay at the head table. Their chances of seeing the woman, let alone recognizing her, were extremely slim. She just wanted the woman to be at her wedding. It was selfish of her, yes, but it was always the little sister's hope that her lost sister would somehow be at her wedding. This was her only chance.

The nurse, after much deliberation, reluctantly agreed to bring up the idea of attending to her adopted daughter. If the woman and her family already had plans for the week of the wedding, there was nothing the little sister could do. The nurse would attend regardless as a sign of trust and good faith. But if the woman was unable to attend, then they would continue as they had planned. The cover story was that despite being states apart, because the little sister was a lawyer, she sometimes had to consult with specialists outside her area to get all the facts she needed to win a case. After many years of service, the nurse was now a highly revered individual in her line of work, and one such case led to the lawyer needing her advice on a certain matter. Through their interactions, the two had become close friends and kept in contact even after the case was closed. Now that the lawyer was getting married, she wanted the nurse to attend as her friend, and she even added a plus-one option in case the nurse wanted to bring someone along.

That was the story they gave to the woman.

The woman agreed to attend the wedding.

On the day of the wedding, both the nurse and the lawyer were quite anxious. The lawyer hoped desperately that her wedding would go off without a hitch, and she and the nurse both prayed that the woman would not notice her blood family. The lawyer had even gone so far as to request that her lost sibling not be mentioned in any of the toasts or speeches her family and friends would give later. She wanted this time in her life to be one of new beginnings, not of longing for the past.

That's why she wanted the woman there. To see her one last time and then move on.

When the nurse and woman arrived, the nurse made sure to seat the two of them in the middle of the sanctuary, opposite of where the bride's family sat. Minutes before she was set to walk down the aisle, the sister opened the door just enough to spot the woman in the crowd, and she wept. Her mother thought they were nervous, happy tears, and she wasn't half wrong. Her lost sister was at her wedding, where she was about to marry the love of her life. The little sister couldn't be happier. Fixing up her makeup and hair one last time, the door opened, and to the little sister's utter joy, her eyes were only on her groom the entire way down the aisle.

The wedding, indeed, went off without a hitch. The lawyer was now a married woman. Toasts, cheers, and the cutting of the cake happened quickly, it seemed, once the reception started. Then it was time for the lawyer and her new husband to lead the first dance. When the merriments were fully underway, the new couple made their rounds to greet all their out-of-town guests. They came up to the nurse and woman, and it took every ounce of the lawyer's professionalism to look only to the nurse first and greet her with a welcoming hug. As they planned, the two exchanged pleasantries before the nurse introduced the bride to the woman.

Shaking the woman's hand, the lawyer saw nary a sign of the sister she'd once known. The barest hint she could see lay in the red scarf the woman had wrapped around her neck; her favorite color was the only thing that didn't change when the woman lost her memory. There was no recognition in the woman's eyes as she told the bride how beautiful her dress was, no wayward glances at the bride's family as if they stirred any sort of memory. The woman's hair had been dyed a different color, and her skin more tanned from years of outdoor activity. Even her posture was different. She was a perfect stranger to the lawyer. As the lawyer turned to her family and watched her brother dance with his girlfriend with their child between them and their parents watching them all with fondness, she knew she'd made the right choice.

Once the wedding ended, the two families went their separate ways. The lawyer went on her honeymoon, content to live with her husband with peace of mind while she furthered her career, spoiled her brother's child, and helped see her parents through their golden years. The nurse saw her adopted daughter off at the airport, checked on her other foster kids as she travelled home, and contemplated getting the papers to adopt another child she had connected well with at the hospital. As for the woman, she went home to her husband and kids, living each day of her life being thankful for the home she'd made for herself and never knowing that she'd spent an entire evening in the same room as her family. She would never know her blood family in the same way the lawyer would never truly know her sister. They both lived their lives that way.

This is the story that runs through my head every time I think about that red scarf. Every month when the tornado sirens are tested, every year when the storm season shows off nature's destructive power, I am reminded of the scarf I saw blowing from the tree branch all those years ago. Of the girl who lost her memory and her home, the nurse who took her in, and the little sister who never gave up searching for the girl.

And this story gives me hope, because though the girl and her family lost so much in that tornado, the storm was not what defined their lives. Was it a major turning point in their lives? Absolutely. But the world kept turning, they kept living, and they thrived. The girl could have wallowed away in pity about her predicament, but she didn't. Instead, she moved forward and made a new family for herself that she could find support and pride in. The lawyer could have spent all her days obsessing over the fate of her sister, but she didn't. Instead, she worked hard and built her way up to the point where her life was stable enough that she could take a moment and find the closure she needed to let go of the past. And the nurse? The nurse could have let that lost young girl fade into the foster system, but she didn't. She offered her home to the girl who couldn't remember her own and gained a daughter as a result.

I don't mean to undermine people and families who have really lost someone to a natural disaster. Nature is a great and destructive force that has and will tear apart countless families for as long as the earth remains. But it's stories like this one that give me hope, hope that our pasts are not what define us. My scars are not easily seen by the naked eye, but they are still there. And once people learn of the kind of scars I have, many judge me for it. But my scars do not define me. My kindness, my resilience, and my faith are only the beginning of what defines who I am and who I can be. I accept and grow from my past, but it does not define me.

What about you? What are you letting define your life? Do you have any hope that you can change? Look outside. It may be cloudy now. It could be snowing or raining, maybe even storming. But the world's still turning, morning still comes, and you are alive.

So where do you put your hope today?

MY DEFEAT, MY VICTORY

I stand dismayed with my mouth agape,
Protected by the lion's paw,
While the jackdaw jitters and diddles
With shrewdness and acuity,
Facing my defeat.
In horror, I watch the lightning clash
And wonder what went wrong.
We'd led the way, placed the signs perfectly,
Set forth the knowledge that would
Start the healing fire
And save our precious world.
Yet still, even my friends became lost.
They left me on the way.
I finished the path alone.
And the once-lightful souls
Have lost their carefree traits.
"Misery, misery, their souls will find,"
The jackdaw cackled.
"The hardest path followed, they must be remind!"
How cruel, I think,
Though the fowl only speaks the truth.
The road was mapped, the way paved.
It was hard.
But all they had to do was follow it.
Yet they ignored it and were led astray.
"Save them, save them, you could not.
Now their souls must be left to rot."
I weep.
It isn't my place to help them anymore.

Turning from the chaos,
From the jackdaw and death,
I reach for the light
And welcome my victory.
"Safe, safe, you sit with the King.
Believer, you are, so forever you'll sing."

CHANGE

New again, new again.
Where to start when we've just began?
Changing, changing, the constant turn.
If you stop, then never you'll learn.
Frighten you, that which the change does succeed.
But was it not by change that the captive's made free?
And yet there, through it all, stands the one solid rock,
Steady, unchanging, unyielding against the clock.
Shifting sand or the ever-steady stone,
What is the answer you feel deep in your bone?
Change is inevitable; to live is to die.
But upon this solid rock is the life I live by.

THE MONSTER UNDER MY BED

I remember the monster
Underneath my bed.
He was so much nicer than
The monsters in my head.
Every time I cried, he was the one
To hold my hand.
But every morning he'd disappear
To the dreadful monster land.
Every time I screamed, he'd roar
For everyone to hear.
Then they'd think for that which I screamed
Was not the thing I feared.
When I went to go, he held me back
And kept me from running away.
He held me close, hugged me tight,
And told me I'm okay.
So the monster under my bed, you see,
Is not the nightmare feared,
But a companion very dear to me,
A friend I most revered.
In the dark, all through the night,
He saw the darkest part of me.
And he became the only one
I knew would never leave.
So ask me about my monster,
And I'll tell you this as fact,
I'd relive my whole dark childhood
Just to get my monster back.

ACKNOWLEDGMENTS (IN A SENSE)

I'll be honest, this section was originally going to be a reflection, but I genuinely didn't know what to say. At the time I'm writing this, I am about eighteen months late turning in my manuscript, and I am both proud that it is finally finished and ashamed that it took me so long. The stories I wanted to share, the messages I wanted to convey, I can only hope that they came through properly in the work God has made through me. This, my *Sea of Symphony*, has become more than I imagined it could be, more than I had come to aim for. The only goal I made for myself was to reach sixty pages, and if things are designed as I have planned, this page is number 59. It's not exactly to my goal, but it's close enough that I feel satisfied. But if I somehow manage to exceed my goal, then praise God, from whom all blessings flow!

Anyway, I'm calling this portion of my book "Acknowledgments" because there are people I want to thank. I will not use full names because I honestly don't have permission to. But I still want these people to know, when they read this, that I am truly thankful for their places in my life. If not for them, if not where God placed them for me, I truly believe I would not be who I am today. And I certainly would not be here for you, my dearest reader, writing my stories for you now.

To start off with, I want to thank my soul sister, Toya. She is one of the truest friends I have ever known, and her insight, love, and passion have helped me to grow more as a person than my younger self ever thought possible. She has helped me to gain confidence in myself, learn to stand up for myself, and learn when I need to let go. Another friend of mine that I need to show appreciation for is *T*, who's acceptance and consideration has gotten me through many dark days. I am very thankful every single day that God put me on the path to meet you both.

Next, I want to thank Missy, Neesha, and Eliana, all three of whom took their time to read and critique my work. When I felt that completing my book was beyond hope and was ready to give it up, they encouraged me to keep going, to get it done. Without them, I wouldn't be at this point here, just a paragraph away from finally reaching that sixtieth page. And their insight on my work, particularly on the stories "Your Mother" and "The Red Scarf," was just the drive I needed to complete it. Those stories are a little different from the versions you read, ladies, but I hope you still enjoyed reading them and that I made you proud. "The Red Scarf," especially, took me a long while to figure out.

Thanking all my coworkers, customers, and managers from the Shoppe where I work is the least I can do. The overflowing amount of kindness and compassion I see in all of you gives me hope for the future. It helps me to believe that I really may have a future. It sounds simple, and a little cheesy, but it's something I still felt needs to be said, because you are all so equally and wonderfully blessed. And I'm very thankful that God put me with you all so that I may witness it.

Okay, now that I'm done tearing up, the next people I want to show gratefulness for are my church family. They are the tech group I volunteer with, the book group I study with, and the prayer group I pray with. The time I've spent with all of you and the discussions we've shared have helped me to grow spiritually in the body of Christ, and to learn and experience the love and trust of God that I have always longed for. God's direct influence is the inspiration for my books, and you all helped me never to lose sight of that. I am grateful and proud to be with you today.

This next part is a shout-out to my youngest sister, whose blunt philosophies helped me to figure out a lot of the hypothetical what-ifs of many of my stories. To my brother, who always made sure I got to church when I needed to be, and to my other sister, who lives out of town now, I'm really, really proud of all of you. I hope you three never doubt how much I love you.

I want to thank my parents as well. They don't always understand the situations I go through, but they do the best they can by me, regardless. Especially my dad. You have no idea how much God has reached me through you throughout my life. I love you both!

I want to take a moment to remember my late grandfather, who passed away in December of 2020. I may not have known him as well as my cousins did, but I am grateful for the time I had with him. And for my grandparents, who still pray for me today, thank you. I really, genuinely, hope that I'm making you proud.

Last and most important, I thank my God. He is the reason I have my stories, my friends, my people, my family, and my life. I have been given stories and dreams—both spiritual and mythical—full of wonder and realism. He is my inspiration and my hope, and I greatly look forward to what He will do in me next.

This is not the end for us, my dear reader. God has plans for us to meet again, though I know not how long it will take. See you again in the Old Oak Tree.

Printed in the United States
by Baker & Taylor Publisher Services